MY FIRST BOOK

ISRAEL

ALL ABOUT ISRAEL FOR KIDS

Copyright 2023 by Globed Children Books

All rights reserved. No part of this book may be reproduced or distributed in any form without prior written permission from the author, with the exception of non-commercial uses permitted by copyright law.

Limited of Liability/Disclaimer of Warranty: The publisher and author make no representations or liabilities with respect to the accuracy and completeness of the contents of this work and specifically disclaim all warranties including without limitations warranties of fitness of particular purpose. No warranty may be created or extended by sales or promotional materials. This work is sold with the understanding that the publisher and author is not engaging in rendering medical, legal or any other professional advice or service. Further, readers should be aware that websites listed in this work may have changed or disappeared between when this work was written and when it is read.

Interior and cover Design: Daniel Day
Editor: Margaret Bam

For My Sons, Daniel, David and Jude

Tel Aviv Coastline, Israel

Israel

Israel is a **country**.

A country is land that is controlled by a **single government**. Countries are also called **nations, states, or nation-states**.

Countries can be **different sizes**. Some countries are big and others are small.

Jerusalem, Israel

Where Is Israel?

Israel is located in the continent of **Asia**.

A continent is **a massive area of land that is separated from others by water or other natural features**.

Israel is situated in the **Western part of Asia.**

Jerusalem, Israel

Capital

The capital city of Israel is Jerusalem.

Jerusalem is located in the **western part** of the country.

Jerusalem is the largest city in Israel.

Tower of David, Jerusalem, Israel

Districts

Israel is divided into six administrative districts

The six districts of Israel are

1. **Jerusalem District**
2. **Northern District**
3. **Haifa District.**
4. **Central District**
5. **Southern District**
6. **Judea and Samaria Area (also known as the West Bank)**

Population

Israel has a population of around **9.7 million people** making it the 91st most populated country in the world.

The population of Israel is highly urbanized, with around 93% of the population living in urban areas. The largest cities in Israel are Tel Aviv, Jerusalem, and Haifa.

Haifa, Israel

Size

Israel is **22,072 square kilometres** making it the 149th largest country in the world by area.

Despite its small size, Israel is a geographically diverse country, with a range of landscapes including mountains, valleys, and deserts. The highest point in Israel is Mount Meron, which stands at 1,208 meters above sea level.

Israeli Child

Languages

The official language of Israel is **Hebrew.** Modern Hebrew is spoken by about nine million people, counting native, fluent and non-fluent speakers. Most speakers are citizens of Israel.

Arabic is a recognised language of Israel

Here are a few phrases in Hebrew
- **Good night - lai-la tov (לילה טוב)**
- **Thank you very much - to-da ra-ba (תודה רבה)**
- **You're welcome - al lo da-var (על לא דבר)**

The Western Wall, Israel

Attractions

There are lots of interesting places to see in Israel.

Some beautiful places to visit in Israel are

- **Masada National Park**
- **Church of the Holy Sepulchre**
- **Bahai Garden Haifa**
- **Western Wall**
- **Caesarea National Park**

Capernaum, Israel

History of Israel

Israel has a long and fascinating history that dates back thousands of years. The history of Israel dates back to biblical times, with the Hebrew Bible describing the Israelites as the chosen people of God.

In the 16th century, the Ottoman Empire conquered Israel and it remained under Ottoman rule until the end of World War I.

Israel declared its independence in 1948

Customs in Israel

Israel has many fascinating customs and traditions.

- **Judaism is the dominant religion in Israel and many Israeli people observe Jewish traditions, including Shabbat, Bar/Bat Mitzvah and Tu Bishvat.**
- **Israeli people love to celebrate! One of the largest celebrations in Israel is Israel's Independence Day, celebrated on the fifth day of the Jewish month of Iyar, it's a time for parades and fireworks. Mimouna is another popular celebration in Israel, which is a traditional Maghrebi Jewish celebration dinner that is held the day after Passover.**

Music of Israel

There are many different music genres in Israel such as Jewish music, Folk music, Klezmer, Middle Eastern music and Mizrahi music.

Some notable Israeli musicians include
- Aviv Geffen: An Israeli rock musician, singer, songwriter and the son of writer and poet Yehonatan Geffen.
- Esther Ofarim: An Israeli singer who came second in the 1963 Eurovision Song Contest.

Food of Israel

Israeli food is known for being tasty, delicious and flavoursome.

The national dish of Israel is **Falafel** which is a delicious dish made of a mixture of ground chickpeas and spices, which are then formed into balls that are then deep-fried.

Hummus

Food of Israel

Israel has a diverse and rich culinary culture influenced by Jewish, Arab, Mediterranean, and Middle Eastern cuisines.

Some popular dishes in Israel include

- **Hummus - A dip made from mashed chickpeas, tahini, lemon juice, and garlic.**
- **Shakshuka - A dish made from eggs poached in a spicy tomato and pepper sauce.**
- **Sabich - A sandwich made with fried eggplant, hard-boiled eggs, Israeli salad, and tahini sauce in pita bread.**

Dome Of The Rock, Jerusalem, Israel

Weather in Israel

Israel has a largely Mediterranean climate, characterized by hot, dry summers and cool, rainy winters. However, due to its diverse topography, the climate varies across the country.

In the coastal region, the summers are humid and the winters are mild and rainy and in the interior regions, the summers are hot and dry, and the winters are cooler and often snowy.

Caracal

Animals of Israel

There are many wonderful animals in Israel.

Here are some animals that live in Israel

- **Caracal**
- **Camel**
- **Arabian oryx**
- **Striped hyena**
- **Nubian ibex**

Eretz Israel Museum

Museums

There are many beautiful museums in Israel which is one of the reasons why so many people visit this beautiful country every year.

Here are some of Israel's Museums

- **The Israel Museum, Jerusalem**
- **Tel Aviv Museum of Art**
- **Eretz Israel Museum**
- **Yad Vashem**
- **Madatech**

Israeli football fan

Sports in Israel

Sports play an integral part in Israeli culture. The most popular sport is **Football.**

Here are some of famous sportspeople from Israel

- **Gal Fridman - Windsurfing**
- **Yael Arad - Judo**
- **Ariel Ze'evi - Judo**
- **Linoy Ashram - Gymnastics**
- **Artem Dolgopyat - Gymnastics**

Chaim Weizmann

Famous

Many successful people hail from Israel.

Here are some notable Israeli figures

- **David Ben-Gurion - Former Prime Minister**
- **Chaim Weizmann - Former President**
- **Yitzhak Rabin - Politician**
- **Natalie Portman - Actress**
- **Golda Meir - Politician**
- **Menachem Begin - Politician**

Nazareth, Israel

Something Extra...

As a little something extra, we are going to share some lesser known facts about Israel

- **Israel is home to the Dead Sea which is the lowest point on Earth.**
- **Israel has the highest number of museums per capita in the world.**
- **Jerusalem, Israel's capital, is one of the oldest cities in the world and is considered holy by Jews, Christians, and Muslims alike.**

Caesarea, Israel

Words From the Author

We hope that you enjoyed learning about the wonderful country of Israel.

Israel is a country rich in culture and beauty, with lots of wonderful places to visit and people to meet.

We hope you continue to learn more about this wonderful nation. If you enjoyed this book, consider leaving a review!

With Love

Made in the USA
Coppell, TX
24 April 2025